eCom Deli

CW00666438

HOW YOUR DELIVERY STRATEGY CAN INCREASE YOUR SALES

Chloë **Thomas**

Print edition published 2015, Kernu Publishing
Originally published in 2014 as an ebook

Kernu Publishing
PO Box 740
Truro
Cornwall
TR1 9HE
United Kingdom

ISBN paperback: 978-0-9926612-1-2
ISBN ebook: 978-0-9926612-2-9

Cover photograph: © Jacqueline Cross Photographer
www.jacquelinecrossphotography.com

Cover and interior design: Visual Philosophy
www.VisualPhilosophy.com

Illustrations: Joni McPherson, McPherson Graphics
www.McPhersonGraphics.com

Photographs, author's own.
Printed in the United Kingdom by TJ International, Cornwall, UK

Praise for *eCommerce Delivery*

. . . .

'This short, concise book is packed full of little nuggets offering solutions to all your delivery dilemmas. Chloë explains how small changes to your delivery processes can lead to significant growth in customer conversion and satisfaction. *eCommerce Delivery* is essential reading for all online product businesses from solo entrepreneurs to large corporate enterprises.'

Karen Faulkner-Dunkley
www.kfdjewellery.co.uk

'At last a book on eCommerce that addresses the key issue of getting your goods to your customers! Well researched, and easy to read this should be required reading for anybody involved in eCommerce!'

John Harvey: logistics guru at 3B International
www.3Bint.co.uk

'Very, very helpful. I'll use it and refer to it a lot in the future.'

Amazon 5-star review

'As a small business we consider ourselves to be fairly good at the general sales and customer service side of things however, as virtually all of our business is Internet-based we realised that we had to promote ourselves more on the Internet and social media platforms but had no idea on how to do this. We discovered the *eCommerce Delivery* book when searching for help on the Internet and it has been brilliant. It has helped us to understand how selling on the Internet really works and has given us many tips that will hopefully allow us to stay ahead of the game. We constantly refer to this book and the other eCommerce books Chloë has written, which are so informative and have definitely been worth every penny.'

Derek and Jenny Brigden, Aerial Balls
AerialBalls.com

'Chloë Thomas cracks it again. Her intelligent, pragmatic advice manages to bring clarity to subjects that are often made too complicated by other experts. I enjoy her natural, free-flowing writing style, which helps the reader to take in the salient points. Great one, Chloë.'

Rob Smeddle, Clientbase Fulfilment
cbfulfilment.co.uk

Why a Book on Delivery?

. . . .

I'm often out and about speaking at eCommerce events and nine times out of ten I will be asked something about delivery; it really is the most regular question. Yet despite the impact of delivery on eCommerce businesses there are almost no books on the subject, so I thought I should write one. (Ten minutes of searching on Amazon gave me two heavy-duty textbooks on logistics, both retailing at over £20.)

In eCommerce, how you get the product to the customer is a really important part of the puzzle. It can be summed up in one word as 'delivery', and when I talk about delivery I mean every aspect of it – how the customer perceives it, as well as how you can use it to increase retention and improve margins and efficiency.

Research undertaken around the world has consistently shown delivery as a top cause of failure to purchase (57% of baskets were abandoned due to delivery, (*Royal Mail Delivery Matters* 2014)). Contributing factors were the cost of it and the convenience of the options available, which means getting your delivery right has a massive impact on your conversion rates. Get it right and see your sales thrive. Let's face it, we've all seen the impact of a free P&P weekend.

This counts across the eCommerce business structures too – how you treat P&P and delivery on Amazon, eBay, etc. is arguably more important than on your own website, as it is a critical part of getting the sale ahead of the competition. By changing the P&P settings on eBay, one of the eCommerce MasterPlan inner circle members increased sales by 20%.

From the customer's point of view it's all about price and convenience. So to get the sale, you need to get the price right, but also provide the convenience your customer requires.

Look at Next, Screwfix, Ironmongery Direct – just how late in the day can we order and still get it delivered tomorrow? At the time of writing (July 2014) the latest we've found is 10 pm. This speed of delivery is such a powerful message it's being used front and centre in marketing materials across the board. The right delivery message (be it convenience or price) is powerful marketing.

Most eCommerce businesses can't hope to meet those levels of delivery speed, but is that what customers want? What's most important to your customers? The speed of delivery, or the price of delivery? Or is it the convenience?

Once the customer has purchased, what should those parcels look like? How secure do they need to be? How pretty? How well branded? Should you put in a voucher to encourage repeat purchase or should you sell space in the parcels to earn some extra cash? Just a cardboard box doesn't cut it anymore. Get it right and you'll even get your customers videoing it and putting it on YouTube – create some excitement and don't forget to match the customer experience across your sales channels from your parcels to your shops.

Of course all delivery costs money – so what's your profit strategy for it? Are you willing to lose money on your postage? How much can you afford to spend to make sure customers get their package as promised, not broken, or late?

Delivery is a subject that affects your whole business. Do it right and it will improve customer acquisition, customer retention, internal efficiency **and** profit. Do it badly and you will lose customers, waste money on marketing, and deal with endless headaches.

In this book I'm going to take you through these key areas of delivery and show you your options. Helping you to find the right strategy for your business.

Successful delivery =

- Meets the customers' hygiene factors to get this order.
- 'Wows' the customer in order to get the next order.

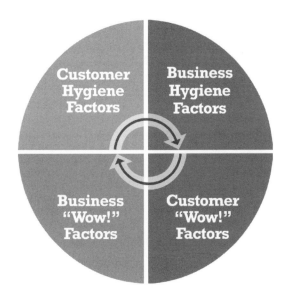

Hygiene factors are things you expect to happen automatically, without you having to check or ask. When you order a cup of coffee, hygiene factors are: the mug, it's hot, it's tasty. The 'wow' factors are what you aren't expecting: a biscuit on the side, or a lovely chat with the waiter.

Customer hygiene factors include:

- the product arrives on time
- for a reasonable price
- in perfect condition
- the delivery options are at a fair price
- and the convenience of delivery is as I want it to be

Business hygiene factors include:

- it all happens efficiently
- costs are within what you can afford

Customer 'wow!' factors include:

- perfect convenience
- low hassle delivery

Business 'wow!' factors include:

- supports your brand
- encourages the next purchase
- increases customer loyalty
- generates social media/PR noise

This book on delivery is here to help you succeed in all those areas.

Contents

. . . .

How to Use this Book

· ·

This book is designed so you can dip in and out of it.

- Need to improve your conversion rate? – it's Part 1 for you.
- Focusing on parcels this month? – try Part 2.
- Need a new courier? – Part 3 will help you.

eCommerce delivery is constantly changing, so the book is designed to help you take the right approach no matter what changes. Of course, you'll need to keep up to date with what's happening and how to use each of the tools: that's where **eCommerceMasterPlan.com** comes in, and throughout the book you'll find the following symbols when there's useful content available for you online:

WORKBOOK

I have created a workbook to help you make the most of this book – so make sure you download it to work through as you read. To get the workbook right now, just go to: **eCommerceMasterPlan.com/Free**

I've also designed a survey especially for readers of *eCommerce Delivery* that you can use to find out what your customers want from you in the delivery stakes. It's all available at: **eCommerceMasterPlan.com/Free** Either take the Google template, or set it up yourself – full instructions are provided.

DOWNLOAD
I have also put a lot of useful templates and other information on the website ready for you to download and use. Please do make the most of them when you see this logo!

WEBSITE
When there's some great extra content that will help you on the website, we've used this logo.

Before you go any further, register at **eCommerceMasterPlan.com/ Free** so you've got quick access to all the support materials.

Enjoy!

PART 1

Delivery Options – Getting the Order

The first job of your delivery strategy is to get the order.

The wrong delivery information, displayed in the wrong way is a key barrier to conversion – so if you don't get it right, you will be losing sales.

In this part we're going to cover:

- Price of delivery – how much should you charge?
- Speed and convenience – getting the balance right for your customers.
- How to get the message across on your website – making sure you're encouraging the purchase.

Price of Delivery

P&P costs are a big reason customers don't buy from you; people will jump through hoops to avoid paying for postage! A recent survey by UPS found that customers would admit to having done the following to avoid P&P charges:

- 58% added extra items to their basket
- 50% chose the longest transit time

- 47% searched for a promotional code
- 35% chose to have the item shipped to store
- 31% joined a loyalty programme to get it
- 30% delayed purchasing until an offer happened
- 16% bought a different product instead to go over the threshold
- only 7% said they did nothing to try and get it

Every business's customers are different, so what works for your business might not work for someone else's.

So what's the right point for your business?

As late as the 2000s, the mail order industry aimed to make a healthy profit on its postage and packing (P&P) charges. So, if the customer paid £4.99, the average cost to the merchant was most likely £4, £3 or even less.

Today, it's hard to find a website that doesn't have free P&P over some level of spend – and the level of spend is getting lower year on year.

You need to decide what your P&P structure is going to be. Making the wrong decision on your P&P charges can be expensive. So be careful to balance customer service with your own profitability.

Remember, for the customer it's a trade-off between convenience and price, and for you it's a trade-off between cost and volume of sales.

There will be a tipping point, a sweet spot, where you get maximum orders at the minimum cost.

DOWNLOAD
At **eCommerceMasterPlan.com/Free** you can download a survey (with instructions) to find out what your customers would value in your delivery options.

Every Business Should Have a Permanent Free Option

(Or at least I have yet to find one that shouldn't!)

This is the simple equation that everything in eCommerce boils down to:

$$\left[\textbf{Traffic}\right] \times \left[\substack{\textbf{Average}\\\textbf{Order Value}\\\textbf{(AOV)}}\right] \times \left[\substack{\textbf{Conversion}\\\textbf{Rate}}\right] = \left[\textbf{Sales}\right]$$

A permanent free P&P offer will help with all three of these:

- Traffic – mention it in adverts and emails to increase visits.
- AOV – if you set it above your normal AOV it will increase spend levels.
- Conversion rate – free P&P increases conversions.

Usually the free option will be the cheapest, with the 'lowest' level of convenience. In the UK it's usually Royal Mail, unsigned 2nd class, arriving in 3–4 days.

As with any promotion, your permanent free P&P's job is:

To get the customer to do what you need them to do, as cheaply as possible.

So the question is, what do you need them to do? And thus what criteria does the customer need to hit to get the reward?

If Your Aim is to Increase AOV

If you want the customer to spend more than they usually would, i.e. increase the Average Order Value (AOV).

First work out your normal AOV and check for any seasonal changes. If it's constant throughout the year then you should set the free P&P rate just above your AOV.

E.g. if your AOV is £50 you set free P&P at £60.

To do this in a more precise way, you want to look at the median rather than the mean average. That means looking at where the spike in orders is and setting the price just above this.

Number of Orders by AOV Band

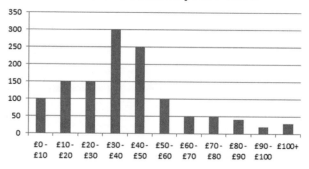

In this case you'd start by setting the P&P threshold at £50 – as you've a big bunch of customers just below that point.

Sometimes it's not that simple though! You may find in your business that you have multiple spikes:

Number of Orders by AOV Band

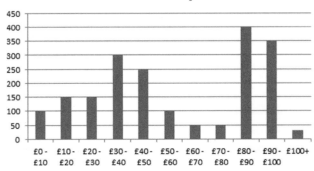

In which case look into the type of products being ordered in each spike. If the upper spike is all furniture purchases then you should include the delivery price within the product price and then you can still put your free P&P threshold at £50.

If Your Aim is Just to Increase Orders

Set your free P&P threshold just below your AOV – this will then appeal to the maximum number of customers without leaving you shipping low-value parcels for free.

So in the above examples, you'd set it at £40 or below.

If You Run a Low Price Point Business

If your AOV is under £10 you may want to just go to free P&P on every order. But if you're going to do this, I suggest you look very carefully at the costs involved before you commit.

If your product can be put straight into a jiffy bag small enough to go through a letter box then your P&P costs are going to be very small, but if you have very bulky or heavy items that need to be delivered and signed off (business cards, personalised stationery, chocolate) then it may be cost prohibitive.

In either case you can always factor an element of the P&P cost into the product cost itself and this can often open up the free P&P opportunity for you.

Should I Go to Totally Free?

Probably not on day one.

It is much easier to lower a free P&P threshold than increase one – so start high and test it for a month and then lower it to see the impact.

For those of you who want to know just how high (or low!) the bar is for free P&P check out ASOS:

FREE DELIVERY WORLDWIDE*
*MORE INFO HERE ›

Which is generally on anything over £15.

But with a permanent 100% free P&P offer, you rob yourself of the promotional opportunity of a free P&P weekend – so it may not be in your interests (even if you can afford to do it) to send every order for free, unless you can afford to offer a more convenient delivery for free as a promotion.

After You've Set Your Free P&P Level – What Next?

Generally, consumers are happy to pay for more speed or convenience. You need to work out which is more important for your customers.

DOWNLOAD

At **eCommerceMasterPlan.com/Free** you can download a survey (with instructions) to find out what your customers would value in your delivery options.

Once you understand what they want you can build your paid delivery options. This is usually a good place to start:

Name of Delivery	Price	Speed	Convenience	Qualifying Criteria?	Which courier?
Free P&P	Free	2-4 days	No signature required	Spend over £50	Acme Cheap - option 1
Standard	£3.99	2-4 days	No signature required	Spend under £50	Acme Cheap - option 1
Next Day	£4.99	The next working day after you order	Signature required	Order by 2pm	Xyz Courier - option B

DOWNLOAD

You can download this as an excel template at:

eCommerceMasterPlan.com/Free

Don't forget to check what the competition is providing and charging, and make sure it fits with your P&P profit strategy.

Delivery Subscriptions

If your customers buy frequently, you may want to launch a delivery subscription where customers pay once for unlimited deliveries over a set time period (usually six months or one year).

The most famous is Amazon's Prime service, which has been great for Amazon, while also educating the consumer to accept subscribing for their deliveries.

Can you do this in your business?

First thing to work out is how often your customers are buying from you. If it's only once or twice a year – then it's not going to be worth running a scheme yourself. But if it's every couple of months then it's worth looking into.

Then you should work out if your IT systems can cope with this – so your website will need to recognise your different customers (delivery subscribers or non-subscribers), and provide each with the right postage options. Your payment system will need to be upgraded to handle subscription payments.

Amazon is no longer the only one doing this – the supermarkets in the UK are following suit, with Ocado running a 'Smart Pass' that gives free delivery, an 'at least' 10% discount on shopping and other benefits, with both mid week and anytime options. Sainsbury's have a 'Delivery Pass' available for 6 or 12 months, mid week or anytime, as have ASOS – with 'ASOS premier' – £9.95 for 12 months of unlimited next day delivery to the UK.

Something to smile about

We've combined all the benefits of our Delivery Pass with the discounts of Saving Pass, plus lots more besides. Say hello to our new Smart Pass.

What's included? All the best bits, of course
Smart is... **waving goodbye to delivery charges**
Smart is... **saving at least 10% on your favourite brands**
Smart is... **priority access to Christmas deliveries**
Smart is... **being eligible for product samples**
Smart is... **a subscription to our Ocadolife magazine**
Smart is... **exclusive offers and discounts**
Smart is... **anniversary gifts**

There are two different delivery plans to choose from - Anytime and Midweek - depending on when, or how often, you like to order. Then you simply select whether you'd rather pay for your membership monthly, six-monthly or annually.

So, what are you waiting for? It's time to make your weekly shop something to smile about.

Frequently Asked Questions >

See membership options >

SMART PASS

There are now even groups of companies getting together to form their own co-operative subscription services such as: www.deliverydeals.co.uk

Speed and Convenience of Delivery

Success in delivery is all about meeting the customer's hygiene levels – what they expect to see. And **generally** they want an option that offers them convenience.

Convenience might mean:

- how quickly the parcel gets to them
- when it gets to them
- how it gets to them

What you need to understand to create the right delivery options for your customers is which of these is the key concern!

This will vary by product sector as well as by demographics. For example:

- If you run a weekly veg box delivery:
    - Your customers don't want to have to be in for your delivery each week.
    - You need a system for where it gets delivered – doorstep? Coal bunker? Pickup location?
    - You should probably also incorporate the cost of delivery into the price of the subscription.
- If you are a big supermarket delivering groceries:
    - Customers want to choose exactly when you deliver to them. Ideally to the shortest time slot possible.
    - They're generally happy to pay extra for more popular slots.
    - Be careful because if you don't arrive within the slot, they won't be happy.
- If you are a gift retailer sending a lot of deliveries direct to gift recipients:
    - I'll bet your customers would like to select delivery dates – see Interflora!
- If you're just a normal eCommerce business:
    - What do your customers want most of all?

I am an Amazon Prime customer, but I'll often choose a non-Prime delivery option as Prime usually has to be signed for and I don't like to interrupt my working day in order to answer the door and accept a parcel!

You need to work out what's important for **your** customers, and (more importantly) what they are willing to pay for:

- Speed – next day, and how late can you take that order?
- Weekend deliveries – Saturday and Sundays.

- Time slots – that they choose or you tell them? How long should they be? Fifteen minutes? Half a day?
- Less onerous – normal post vs. signed for courier. A courier where they can inform a safe place?
- Which courier – do they have a preference?

Lookfantastic.com tell the customers which couriers they use as the customer is going through the basket:

◉ Premium Next Day Delivery (DPD) - Monday to Thursday order before 8pm. Sundays and Bank Holidays order before 2pm. Courier will email with 1hr delivery slot. Restrictions apply & excludes Bank Holidays. - £4.95

◎ Standard Next Day and Saturday Delivery (Yodel) - Monday to Friday order before 8pm for delivery the following day. Sundays and Bank Holidays order before 2pm. Restrictions apply & excludes Bank Holidays. - £3.95

◎ Premium Saturday Delivery - Order before 8pm Friday. Courier will email with 1hr delivery slot. Restrictions apply. - £8.95

◎ Standard Delivery - £0.00

There are three ways you can research this, and I recommend doing all three:

1. Analyse existing customer behaviours:
   a. What delivery are they choosing? How many are going for free? Standard? Next day? Etc.
   b. What are they saying to your customer service team/in reviews?
2. Ask the customers:
   a. Run a survey.
   b. Use focus groups if you are large enough to do these (icing on the cake stuff!).
3. Look at the eCommerce leaders/your competition:
   a. Look at your top competitors – what are they offering and promoting?

b. And if they have public reviews – what are their customers saying about the delivery? (Never underestimate how much of a competitor's strategy you can learn by reverse engineering their marketing!)

Once you've got an idea of what they want, it's time to work out if you can deliver it.

- Can you afford to? Often you won't have enough parcel volume to get the best options.
- Can your systems cope – and manage the options in an easy to understand way?

Then – set up what you can and test it out!

I recommend reviewing your options at least every six months.

DOWNLOAD

At **eCommerceMasterPlan.com/Free** you can download:

- a survey (with instructions) to find out what your customers would value in your delivery options
- a template for your research activity report

Here's some new trends that might appeal to your customers.

Convenience Trends – The Ever Later Next Day Option

ORDER **BY 10PM**
FOR DELIVERY TOMORROW

NOW ON **SUNDAYS**
TO HOME FOR £3.99 *OR* FREE TO STORE*

A key trend in the UK (that is in play around the world too) is the ever later next day delivery cut off.

On most websites the customer must order by 12 noon/1 pm (or something similar) to get the parcel the next day. However, this time slot is being pushed ever backwards.

In the UK the hygiene level that customers expect is being continually pushed later by a delivery battle, primarily in the building supplies and fashion sectors.

At the time of writing, the key players in the building trade are offering:

- Ironmongery Direct:
  - Monday to Saturday before 8 pm – next working day.
  - Sunday up to 3.30 pm – next working day.
  - All for **free** on orders over £45.

- Screwfix:
    - Monday to Friday before 7 pm – next working day.
    - Sunday before 2 pm – next working day.
    - Mainly free over £50.

In the less competitive fashion market (where you don't get it for free):

- Next:
    - Order by 10 pm for delivery tomorrow, including Sunday deliveries.
    - Delivered for **free** to a store for collection next day.
    - Other options:
        - Evening deliveries.
        - Same day delivery before 12 noon.
        - 4 day service on furniture for just £3.99.

- ASOS:
    - Order by 10 pm Monday to Friday, free next day delivery when you spend £100 (otherwise £5.95).
    - Order by midnight Monday to Friday, free evening next day delivery when you spend £150 (otherwise (£7.95).
    - Oddly, ASOS require the customer to enter a discount code to get the offer.

How late in the day can you push your next day? Could you fast track specific product ranges? What are your competitors doing?

Convenience Trends – Choose Your Delivery Slot

In the grocery market this is essential – but it is starting to roll out to other eCommerce websites too. At the moment there are a number of different options being trialled – it's going to be interesting to see which one the customer uses the most. Current options we've seen include:

- Pick your day: ASOS allow UK customers to pick a day up to 7 days in advance (including Sunday) for £5.95.
- Sunday deliveries: Many stores are now offering a Sunday, usually at premium price.
- Evening deliveries: There's also a growing trend for offering an evening delivery so the customer doesn't have to stay home from work.

Can you offer delivery slots? What are your competitors doing?

Convenience Trends – Click and Collect

For any business with bricks and mortar locations, a click and collection option is a great way to increase sales.

It's a service which enables customers on your website to either:

- Have their order delivered to a store for them to pick up.
- Reserve stock that's in store already for them to pick up.

For the customer the difference between these is slight, but huge for your systems.

Some businesses use both options, whilst others use just one. Generally if your stores tend to stock your whole range then go for the stock reserving option – in the UK this is particularly popular with the big sheds – Homebase, Argos, PC World, etc. Here, again, speed is also a key factor – with promises of 'collect within one hour'.

If your stores have different stock, or it's too complicated to get store stock onto the website, then why not deliver customer orders to the store? Often this is easier for the customer than having it delivered to home. And if you're a fashion store then they can try on right there and then, immediately returning what doesn't work for them.

Christmas 2013 John Lewis used their Waitrose supermarkets (one of the biggest in the UK) for 'have your order delivered to our stores' – which was too great a success! It led to massive storage issues in the Waitrose supermarkets that were bombarded with John Lewis parcels. So if you're going to test this, don't underestimate the volumes and don't assume the customers will pick up when you want them to!

Of course to do this you do need stores, and you also need integrated systems. What are the options if you don't have your own stores or your stores can't handle it?

Convenience Trends – Click and Collect When You Don't Have Stores

Several UK companies have created a number of pickup locations around the country, which any retailer can deliver their parcels to; giving the customer potentially even greater convenience as they get to pick up parcels sent by multiple merchants from one place.

DOWNLOAD
At **eCommerceMasterPlan.com/Free** you can download a list of the currently available click and collect services.

This is also now turning into something of a land-grab …

Amazon is currently working on a number of deals with Transport for London. Already in action are pickup lockers in Tube station car parks, but they are also rumoured to be working on a deal to lease every ticket office on the Tube network and turn them into parcel collection lockers …

Even if you have your own stores you may want to look at other locations – in June 2014 Sainsbury's (one of the UK's biggest supermarkets) announced that they are launching a click and collect in the car parks of seven London Tube stations. Orders placed by 1 pm will be ready to collect at the end of the commuter's journey home.

How to Get the Message Across on Your Website

Once you've put together the perfect delivery options to maximise conversions by meeting both your and the customer's hygiene factors, it's time to make sure the customer knows about them.

This whole delivery options exercise is about getting the customer to buy more by increasing your conversion rate, so it's really important you make it easy for customers to understand and pick the right option for them.

Make it too complex and it will have the opposite effect – reducing the conversion rate!

This is a big challenge, one that is all solved with clever design.

Homepage

Here you need to shout about how cheap and convenient your postage is.

Your free P&P threshold should be here so should any convenience messages that are important to your customers.

Ideally, put these in the header – so they're seen across the website.

Here are some examples – but look at your competition and other sites you admire to see how they do it.

Delivery Information Page

This is probably the most difficult page on the website to get right, and one we often forget about.

Keep it easy to understand and easy to scan, so customers can quickly find what they want to know, but do make sure to give them all the information they want.

Ironmongery Direct – very clear, I like how they highlight the questions answered by the page right at the top so the customer knows they are in the right place.

The tables make it really easy to understand the options:

Delivery Information

| When will my order be delivered? | How much will delivery cost? |

Delivery Schedule

Monday - Saturday order up to 8:00pm	Sunday order up to 3:30pm	Sunday order after 3:30pm
Next working day *Between 8am ~ 6pm*	Monday *Between 8am - 6pm*	Tuesday *Between 8am - 6pm*

A two-day service will apply to orders placed after 3.30pm in Scotland which contain a product over 1 metre in length. Next day delivery is not available for Republic of Ireland, Scottish Highlands and some remote areas where an additional charge may apply. Please call for further details.

Delivery Costs

Standard Next Day Delivery	
Orders over £45 (excl VAT) FREE	Orders under £45 (excl VAT) £5.95

Delivery Upgrades					
Next working day **Before Noon**		Next working day **Before 10:30am**		Saturday *Between 8am - 6pm*	
Under £45 £8.45	Over £45 £7.50	Under £45 £13.45	Over £45 £7.50	Under £45 £15.95	Over £45 £10.00

Screwfix – I like the use of the map to make expectations for different areas clear. But the rest is confusing and contradictory, which will stop customers from buying.

It promises 'Place your order by 7 pm and we'll deliver to you or your customer the very next day!' but given they've highlighted Saturday as something special – what about Sunday deliveries?

And the fast delivery options have strange names:

- Fast = Standard
- Faster = Premium
- Fastest = premium (lower case p)

Why not just call them 'Fast', 'Faster' and 'Fastest'?

This lack of clarity will prevent orders being placed.

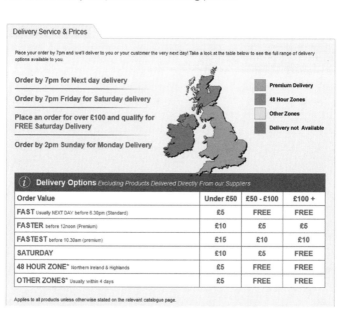

Delivery Service & Prices

Place your order by 7pm and we'll deliver to you or your customer the very next day! Take a look at the table below to see the full range of delivery options available to you.

Order by 7pm for Next day delivery

Order by 7pm Friday for Saturday delivery

Place an order for over £100 and qualify for FREE Saturday Delivery

Order by 2pm Sunday for Monday Delivery

Premium Delivery

48 Hour Zones

Other Zones

Delivery not Available

(i) **Delivery Options** *Excluding Products Delivered Directly From our Suppliers*

Order Value	Under £50	£50 - £100	£100 +
FAST Usually NEXT DAY before 6.30pm (Standard)	£5	FREE	FREE
FASTER before 12noon (Premium)	£10	£5	£5
FASTEST before 10.30am (premium)	£15	£10	£10
SATURDAY	£10	£5	FREE
48 HOUR ZONE* Northern Ireland & Highlands	£5	FREE	FREE
OTHER ZONES* Usually within 4 days	£5	FREE	FREE

Applies to all products unless otherwise stated on the relevant catalogue page.

Next – I thought this was a poor attempt.

It does show me there are lots of options, but to work out which is right for me and the products I'm buying I'd have to click through and follow all the asterisks – not very user friendly.

Delivery Options >

Free Express Next Day Delivery to Store
Order by 10pm for Next Day Delivery to Store* Read More >

Next Day Delivery to Home
NEW Order by 10pm for Next Day Delivery to Home for just £3.99. Now on Sundays* Read More >

Evening Delivery to Home
Out all day? We now offer evening delivery for only £3 more* Read More >

Same Day Delivery to Home
In a hurry? Order by 12 midday and receive your order today* for only £3 more. Read More >

4 Day Delivery - Home Furniture
Speedy 4 day delivery for furniture items* for just £3.99 Read More >

Send to a Friend Service
Not at home during daytime? Want to send a gift? Send your order to a friend or neighbour*.
Read More >

Debenhams – a simple expanding questions format, with clear answers to each question. But to get the full picture I have to click on lots of questions. A table like Ironmongery Direct would be a bonus here.

UK delivery

▼ **How much does delivery cost?**

UK, N. Ireland - FREE on all orders over £30. Delivery is normally charged at £3.99 (e:

Click & Collect - FREE on all orders.

In store ordering - FREE on all orders.(some exceptions apply).

Next Day - £4.99 on all orders.

Republic of Ireland – FREE on order over €30. Delivery is normally charged at €5. Sho

For charges on international delivery, please **click here**.

If you are a Debenhams Gold cardholder, standard UK delivery is free of charge. The automatically at checkout.

▶ Do you deliver to all UK addresses?

▶ How long do standard deliveries take?

▶ How does the Next Day home delivery service work?

▶ What happens if I am out when the courier comes?

▶ Can I order a delivery to go to my place of work, or another address?

▶ What are the normal delivery times?

ASOS – good, clear layout means you can quickly see your options. But the use of discount codes is a bit odd and there is some inconsistency in the text. (E.g. 'Order by 10 pm Monday–Friday (2 pm Sunday)' – what about Saturday?)

A critical page to get right, so spend some time on this one and test if you need to!

Product Pages

The product page is where your customers are making their first buying decision, so you want to remove all questions (reasons not to buy) from their minds and build their trust that you'll deliver the product well.

That means this page should be highlighting:

- delivery speeds
- delivery prices
- stock holding

Speed example from The Present Finder:

Despatch:
Despatch of this item is currently 5 days from the date of ordering

Our price £12.99

Name on Glass : *

12 characters remaining

Required field *

| 1 | Add to Basket | | Add to Wishlist |

Amazon is particularly good at this on the product list page.

eCommerce MasterPlan ·

£5.66 Kindle Edition

Available for download now

~~£9.99~~ **£8.96** Paperback *Prime*

Get it by **Friday, Jul 4**

eCommerce Marketing: H

£5.66 Kindle Edition

Available for download now

~~£9.99~~ **£6.99** Paperback *Prime*

Get it by **Friday, Jul 4**

Only 12 left in stock - order soon.

It's easy to read – all the information is there and it doesn't look ugly or cluttered.

And the same time is the case on the product page:

ECommerce Marketing: How to Drive Traffic That Buys to Your Website (Ecommerce Masterplan) [Paperback]

Chloe Thomas ⊙ (Author)
★★★★★ ⊙ (2 customer reviews)

RRP: £9.99
Price: £6.99 ✓Prime
You Save: £3.00 (30%)

Only 12 left in stock (more on the way).
Dispatched from and sold by **Amazon**. Gift-wrap available.

Want it by 1pm tomorrow, 4 July? Order it within 7 hrs 17 mins and choose **Express Delivery** at checkout. Details

19 new from £4.11   4 used from £6.26

Formats	Amazon Price	New from	Used from
Kindle Edition	£5.66	--	--
Paperback	£6.99 ✓Prime	£4.11	£6.26

A masterclass in how to both reassure the customer, and urge them to buy now! 'Only 12 left in stock (more on the way)'.

Not on the High Street also manage this rather well:

Smartphone Projector
by LUCKIES
£15.95 ★★★★☆
3 customer reviews

IN STOCK

- **£2.75** mainland UK delivery - Order now and receive this item on or before **Monday 7 July**

- **£7.70** Express Next Day - Order now and receive this item on or before **Monday 7 July**

- International Delivery Available

quantity
[1]
ADD TO BASKET

Bureau Direct sell stationery, and all their orders over £5 are free P&P, but they still hammer it home:

£2.50

Stock item
Free UK Delivery over £5
Brand: Whitelines
Code: WL/WL50
MPN: WL50

Stock Status: Stock item

Qty 1

Add to Basket

Of course in fashion you need to display the sizing stock too, ECCO Shoes do this simply and effectively:

Biom Golf

£ 180.00 100013

Colours

Size

35 36 37 38 39 40 41

Show sizes in: EU UK US

Key: in stock   low on stock   stock in soon   online only   out of stock

Quantity 1   ADD TO BAG

designed based upon the
profile platform, with a wider
ility bars between each

THIS ITEM
QUALIFIES FOR
FREE DELIVERY

id additional fraction bars.

Checkout

Often when you service your customers' delivery needs well your delivery options will either reduce to one (free P&P for all) **or** a complex suite of options.

So it's critical you make it easy to understand.

If you're selling internationally, try and identify the country asap so you can get the right kind of prices upfront instead of waiting till after a country is selected.

Here are some examples of making the complex easy – it might take a little bit of design and systems tweaking, and you won't get it right first time, but spend the time and it will be worth it.

Amazon is the master of this – with each of its marketplace sellers being able to offer different delivery options you would think it'd struggle, but the delivery options are so intuitive and easy to use:

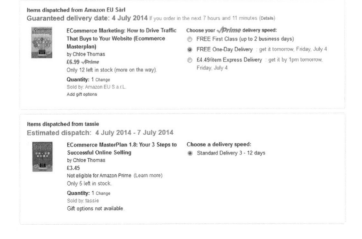

As is TheTrainline.com:

Select a Delivery Option

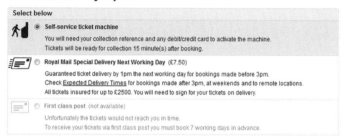

Although they almost certainly lose orders because they make you fill out this section:

Having to choose a station despite the technology being such that, in reality, you can pick up from anywhere! Unnecessary steps will cost you orders.

What makes it even worse, if you click continue without your starting station selected they give you this long-winded and pointless error message:[1]

---

1 I spend a lot of time on trains, in fact this book was mainly written on First Great Western between Reading and St Austell! Thanks to the team on the trains for the endless peppermint teas and almond croissants.

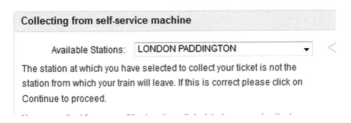

So be careful to keep your delivery options simple and straightforward in the checkout so you don't distract customers from checking out!

Rest of the Site

Don't underestimate the power of microtext.

Microtext is a little line of text that gets straight to the point. So it could be 'next day available until 1 pm' under the add to basket button.

Or 'choose your delivery slot' under the perpetual basket in the header.

It's not designed, it's not clever – it's very simple and very effective.

Look through the whole site and work out where you can encourage the customer to make that buying decision.

If you have customers buying for specific dates, have somewhere you can highlight those last order dates across the website.

E.g. 'Father's Day Last Orders 2 pm Thursday'.

Adds a nice extra bit of reassurance.

NOTES

Post Purchase Delivery – It's Time to **Wow!** the Customer and Get the Next Order

PART 2

Now you've got the order, the next job of your delivery strategy is to impress the customer so that they buy again. How can the parcel build brand loyalty and directly encourage the next purchase?

You need to deliver the parcel in a way that satisfies all the customers' expectations (their hygiene factors) **and** wows them a little bit. A perfect parcel is a mixture of what the customer wants, and what you want …

In this part we're going to cover:

- The customers' perfect parcel – what they expect.
- The eCommerce businesses perfect parcel – how to make it work for you, including wowing the customer.
- A little bit about returns – a very important aspect for the customer.

The Customer's Perfect Parcel

Please don't be lulled into a false sense of security by the short length of this section!

The customer's perfect parcel is based on these hygiene factors:

- Arrives on time.
- Arrives in good condition.
- Arrives with the goods in perfect condition.
- Arrives with the right paperwork.
- If there's a wow factor – cool, but not essential.

Achieving this is not always easy, and a lot of it is outside your direct control.

Take a look at your parcels and couriering – how well are they satisfying the above criteria?

The eCommerce Businesses Perfect Parcel

On the hygiene factor side, the perfect parcel must do all that the customer wants in order to minimise your workload and avoid creating an unhappy customer.

But now you need to make it work for you too. Which means:

- Be cost effective.
- Wow the customer into buying again.

Be Cost Effective

To wow the customer there is a **lot** you can do – but all of it costs a bit. So please, please after you've gotten excited, and before you buy a lot of tissue paper and custom envelopes – **cost it out**!

There may be some elements you'll be able to afford once you grow a bit more – so spend on the most impactful ones first and, of course, don't forget to test!

Ideas for Wowing the Customer With Your Parcels ...

There are lots of ways you can wow the customer with your parcel. Remember the aim is to build brand awareness to increase the likelihood of the next sale, or even to get them to recommend you to their friends.

The Outer Packaging

It all starts with the outer packaging. This is a great opportunity to reinforce your brand.

- Can you brand the address label?
- Have custom packaging designed?

If you can – what do you want that message to be?

Lovefilm always use their envelopes to show their expertise in film and TV, and then either to encourage greater interaction with their service, or sometimes as advertising for films in the cinema.

Schuh use theirs to highlight their range of branded footwear – simple and effective.

The Hut Group use the same boxes across all their stores – encouraging customers to shop from several of their websites.

Creating custom boxes is not cheap – so if you only ship a few items how can you do this cost effectively?

I love this example from Lawless Denim – they're an American company who make custom jeans, which arrive in a simple cardboard box with a stamp of their logo on it.

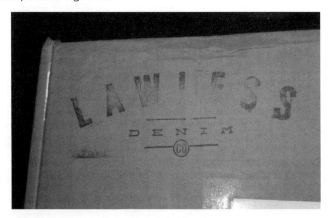

The slight imperfection in the stamp suits their industrial image, and this is a very cheap way to add that bit of excitement to the delivery. Can you use a stamp? Or would you prefer to use a sticker? Both are very cheap and easy options.

Don't Do Bubble Wrap Overkill

Or packaging overkill – there's a company I regularly order make-up from. They send it out in a padded jiffy bag with their logo on (great), then the individual make-up items are wrapped in tissue paper and endless bubble wrap and a lot of sellotape. It's overkill, an eye shadow isn't going to break in a jiffy bag. Every time they arrive I have to sit down with the scissors and spend a few minutes (seriously!) unpicking the parcel.

This is frustrating for the customer and wasteful, and expensive for the retailer – both in terms of time to pack, packaging supplies and postage due to the extra weight.

What is in the Parcel?

This is where you really want to wow them. If you do a good job, they'll put you all over social media for it.

WEBSITE

Go to **eCommerceMasterPlan.com/Free** to find out more about the unboxing trend – where customers record a video of themselves unboxing the goods and then share it on social media!

What do you already do in your stores, and are you replicating that in the parcels? What else could you do to make the unboxing experience more 'wow'?

Wrap the products in tissue paper, or a special bag. What sort of packaging would fit with your brand? Lawless send out their jeans wrapped in a simple canvas bag using that stamp again:

Can you put in a 'packed by ____' card, for that personal touch? Even if you mass-produce these so that the names are pre-printed it will still add some wow factor!

With the order confirmation: firstly send it as a VAT receipt if you're selling to businesses (personal plea directed mainly at Amazon sellers!); secondly, how much can you brand it and can you put an offer on it?

Can you add a freebie?

An unexpected/surprise gift is always exciting. So is there something small, light, cheap, and on-brand that you can send them?

It might be a funky sticker, a packet of seeds, or a good luck charm. Something that fits with your brand.

In the USA Blue Chip Wrestling send a free T-shirt out with every order. They print T-shirts for 100s of wrestling events each year and inevitably have lots left over. So they started asking their customers for a T-shirt size as they checkout, and then send them a T-shirt from a past event. The social media noise this generates is huge! And all that noise is a result of very happy customers, and very happy customers buy again.

Direct Calls to Action to Get the Next Sale

Of course within your parcels should also be a direct call to action to ask for the next order!

The point when the customer opens the parcel should be when they love the retailer the most, so it's a great time to ask them to order again. Some ideas:

- Include a catalogue.
- Include a voucher for a discount/P&P free on the next order.
- On the despatch note – include an offer!
- An offer for their friends.

It doesn't need to be complicated or expensive – it could just be a business card sized item, or a postcard.

The Hut Group put in a 12 page mini-magazine, featuring key products and a competition. I would be **very** surprised if the brands featured haven't contributed to the cost of this marketing:

Make Money From Your Parcels

Usually there's a bit of space in your parcel that can be sold, or 'swapped'.

Swapping space means you exchange a number of leaflets with another retailer – they put your leaflets in their parcels, and you put theirs into yours. This can be a very cheap way to recruit new customers.

Alternatively you can sell the space in your parcels – earning on average £100 per 1,000 leaflets inserted. Usually you can sell (or swap) up to four or five spaces in the parcel. So that could be a total of £400 per 1,000 parcels.

With either of these you'll need to factor in the cost of inserting the leaflets – warehouses charge differently for this, so make sure you're clear on the pricing before you start.

And if you're feeling nervous of it – just take a look at your next Amazon parcel.

Returns

Returns is an area where most eCommerce businesses can save money, and improve profit. That means reducing the returns rate. So I had to include a section on this, but as most of the ways to improve returns aren't delivery related – it's a short section!

Making customers pay to return goods to you is a way to reduce the returns rate. But it also reduces a customers' likelihood to buy in the first place, and to buy again!

So you should be offering a free returns service, whether that's via the post office or a courier pickup like several couriers now offer. The easier you make it for the customer to do business with you the more they'll buy.

That means the majority of returns reduction is outside the scope of your delivery – it's about getting the product right, and correctly explained on the website.

However, delivery does still have a part to play:

- Make sure the goods arrive in good condition – if they're damaged they will get returned. The right packaging and the right courier are essential.
- Make sure they arrive fast – to avoid the 'well his birthday was last week, so it's too late and I'm returning them' scenario.
- Wowing the customer to avoid buyer's remorse!

 DOWNLOAD
At **eCommerceMasterPlan.com/Free** you can download a list of returns services.

NOTES

3 Overcome the Internal Challenges to Improve Efficiency

· ·

We've covered working out what you should be doing – but there are challenges to getting it all live and making the added complexity work for you. In this part we'll run through how to approach some of the common internal challenges including:

- Getting it out of the warehouse.
- Outsourcing your warehousing.
- Finding the right courier.
- Involving the whole business.
- The 7 eCommerce business structures key delivery challenges.

Getting It Out of the Warehouse

How quickly you can get the order to the customer is really important and there are two parts to that, how quickly the courier can deliver it **and** how fast you can get it out of your warehouse. You need to have your warehouse operating to deliver a reliable despatch speed.

Twenty-eight days is no longer acceptable. You need to be despatching **fast**.

Consumers are used to speedy delivery and they expect it. Customers probably won't notice that you're stating 28 days (or 7 days) on the website, but when the parcel doesn't arrive as quick as they think it should they're just going to call you, and email you, and Facebook you until it's delivered. This creates unnecessary work and public relations issues, as well as a disappointed customer.

So speed up that warehouse!

Make sure the orders are being picked efficiently and in the right order. Make sure you have enough manpower to pick it all – so you do need to get a handle on predicting volumes.

You Can't Despatch It If It Isn't There

It's very easy to annoy customers by letting them order something that isn't actually in stock, so you need to have accurate stock information, and get that onto the website. Accurate on-site stock information builds trust through transparency, leading to more conversions; and if you can also include when new stock is going to be delivered in order to create the right expectation you'll also see an increase in conversions.

Giving the customers this extra information will also reduce customer service queries.

Not trusting that they'll get the goods is a big issue for customers – a big barrier to conversion. So if you want to make sure your customers buy, tell them on the product page when they're going to receive their orders. (See examples in Part 1.)

Outsourcing Warehousing and Pick, Pack and Despatch

Do what you are good at and hire experts to do the rest.

If you don't think it would be cost effective for you to outsource then you need to look wider than just the financial considerations. How much of your time do you spend picking and packing and dealing with stock? If you could use that time elsewhere in the business what else could you achieve? What is the opportunity cost of doing it in-house?

There is a pick, pack and despatch outsourcing option for every business size. At eCommerce MasterPlan our only physical product is the books, and we've cost effectively outsourced the despatch of these. So if we can do it – so can you! There is no barrier to outsourcing – it doesn't matter how small your volumes are, how complex you think your products are, or what systems you use; there will be an outsourced warehouse for you, and your business will be better for it.

The benefits of outsourcing your warehousing are:

- Faster despatch.
- Often cheaper postage because of the warehouse's economies of scale from adding lots of retailers' parcels together.
- More courier options.
- Less overheads in your business – people, space, systems.
- May enable you to relocate to better offices.
- More flexible resources – go on holiday? Your parcels will still go out. Sudden spike in orders? Everything will still go out on time.
- And most importantly it also saves your time and effort, so you can reinvest in other areas of the business making head office more efficient.

I used to deal with all the book orders from the eCommerce MasterPlan website – it was nice, it gave me an excuse to nip down to St Mawes (pretty seaside village in Cornwall) every few days. But doing it myself meant that I kept interrupting important tasks to look at the orders, or to go to the post office. It also meant customers got a bad experience – if I was in London for a couple of days and orders came in whilst I was away it would be a few days before I could get the books into the post. Which then meant I had to deal with emails of people chasing delivery too. Now I've outsourced the whole piece the customers are getting a better service, and I'm able to plan promotions on the books when they should happen, not to coincide with when I have time to get the orders out!

The key is to find the right warehousing partner for the stage your business is at right now. Don't just look at the warehouses who are near you – it doesn't really make any difference to the service you and your customers will get where the warehouses are. Location can make a big difference to costs though, outlying areas often have cheaper space and lower wages (the two big costs of any pick, pack and despatch service) which means you'll get a lower price. If you're in the UK take a look at Cornwall and Cumbria.

Here's my step-by-step guide to finding that partner:

1. Create a forecast of your parcels by month for the next 12 months, including likely weights and sizes (this can just be an average).
2. And a forecast for the next five years, by year – so you can see if they'll fit in the future.
3. And a forecast of how much stock you'll need them to store for the next 12 months and for the next five years, by year.
4. Create a list of likely overseas volumes, not all warehouses will deal with overseas delivery.

5. Create a list of what services you want to offer your customers (both outbound and inbound parcels).

6. Create a list of what extra services you'll need them to provide – returns, phone calls, how do you want things packed, do you run inserts, what turn around speed do you require, any special storage requirements (frozen or valuable items), do they need to check the quality of parcels being received from suppliers?

7. Work all of this up into a tender document for the warehouses you will be speaking to, which should also include:

   a. Location of your warehouse(s) and stock transfer plans.

   b. Timetable for the switch over.

   c. Key contacts.

   d. Details of the systems you use to manage orders so they can let you know if they can integrate.

   e. Request customer testimonials, ideally for companies of a similar size and with similar products to you.

   f. Do you do wholesale orders?

8. Send the tender document to the warehouses you wish to speak to, and ask them to respond with the prices they can give you. Give them a deadline to get back to you.

9. Privately divide the list into 'must haves' and 'nice to haves'.

10. Privately work out how much you can afford to spend per parcel to hit your margins.

11. Once you have all the tender responses, pick the best ones and meet with them to discuss the opportunity further. I suggest you meet with 2–4.

12. When you select your warehouse of choice do all you can to create a good working relationship with them.

Once you have your new warehouse on board, monitor their performance! And meet with them regularly to find out what new services and developments there are.

DOWNLOAD
You can download a template for a warehouse tender document at **eCommerceMasterPlan.com/Free**

Courier Agreements/Finding the Right Courier(s)

To provide the best choice of delivery to your customers and to get the right price for yourselves you need to have a good relationship with the couriers, and negotiate a good deal.

Good deals usually go to those with volume.

If you don't have volume you're going to struggle to get a good deal (another reason why you should look at outsourcing your pick, pack and despatch).

Often these are worked out on an average weight or by size, so are there some products you should kick into touch because they're having a negative impact on your delivery costs.

1. Create a forecast of your parcels by month for the next 12 months, including likely weights and sizes (this can just be an average).
2. And a forecast for the next five years, by year – sometimes you can negotiate a better deal now based on future growth.
3. Create a list of likely overseas volumes.

4. Create a list of what services you want to offer your customers (both outbound and inbound parcels).
5. Work all of this up into a tender document for the couriers you will be speaking to, which should also include:
   a. Location of your warehouse(s).
   b. Key contacts.
   c. Details of the systems you use to manage orders so they can let you know if they can integrate.
   d. Request for performance KPIs – e.g. how many 'lost in transits', how many parcels delivered first time.
   e. Request for customer testimonials, ideally for companies of a similar size and with similar products to you.
6. Send the tender document to the couriers you wish to speak to, and ask them to respond with the prices they can give you. Give them a deadline to get back to you.
7. Privately divide the list into 'must haves' and 'nice to haves'.
8. Privately work out how much you can afford to spend per parcel to hit your P&P margin targets (which might be to lose money on it, or make money on it).
9. Privately check out the end customers experience – in the UK we're lucky enough to have Money Saving Expert's post-Christmas survey! www.moneysavingexpert.com/news/shopping/2014/01/yodel-named-worst-parcel-delivery-service-again
10. Once you have all the tender responses, pick the best ones and meet with them to discuss the opportunity further. I suggest you meet with 2–4.
11. When you select your courier of choice do all you can to create a good working relationship with them. Of course you might need multiple couriers in order to offer all the delivery options you want.

12. Also, keep a second courier in reserve – so that if your primary courier has a problem, you have a backup ready to go. If you have the volume, you might send 80% of parcels via courier number 1, and 20% via the backup.

Once you have your new courier(s) on board, monitor their performance! And meet with them every 3–6 months to find out what new services and developments there are.

The world of delivery is changing at pace at the moment, so I'd recommend re-tendering every 12 months so you know what options are out there.

DOWNLOAD

You can go to **eCommerceMasterPlan.com/Free** to download:

- a template for a courier tender document
- list of UK couriers

Building a Good Relationship With Your Couriers

This is essential and taking note of a few key things will really help, so with every parcel make sure you're providing the right information:

- full address details
- postcode
- a phone number
- special instructions – i.e. where to leave it if not in

And be realistic. Give them a reasonable lead time to deliver, and have realistic expectations at Christmas and other busy times. There are only going to be so many drivers able to make deliveries, and however much you shout at the courier on the 24th December **your** customers are still going to be let down. Consider getting all your parcels out the day before the last day your couriers have promised – build in the wiggle room to keep the customers happy. Plus, have a backup solution in place for the handful of orders that have issues.

Involve the Whole Business

Getting your delivery options right isn't something that can be done by one department in the business. It's going to involve everyone:

- Marketing – to do the research and work out how to position it all.
- Customer services – involve in the research, and to manage and explain it to customers.
- Buying and merchandising – if it impacts on direct despatch items, the product selection and how products are packaged.
- Shop teams – if you're going to incorporate the shop network.
- Finance – to check out the pricing, margin, etc.
- Warehouse – to negotiate with the couriers.
- Website team – to work out how to integrate it and make the selections easy to do.

If you have people or departments covering each of these within the business or a number of outsourced providers – involve them all.

If there's only one or two of you in the business, then just think it through with all your different hats on before you make the changes!

The Team Includes Those You Are Outsourcing To

Any successful delivery strategy relies on systems of people – pickers, packers, postmen and couriers. You need to build a good relationship with each of those you speak to on a regular basis, as well as those you don't speak to.

These strong relationships will pay off in times of stress when you really need them to go the extra mile for you. When the courier has one last order to drop off on New Year's Eve but it's already 5 pm, human nature means they're more likely to bother if you've put the special instructions in the order so they know they can get it delivered and they recognise your logo and know your parcels are easy. When you know one of your VIP customer's parcels is lost in the depot and you're trying to persuade your depot rep to go and look for it. When the packer notices a typo on one of your parcel inserts you want them to be bothered to tell you and not turn a blind eye.

You will need people to go beyond their job roles for you – and that will only happen if you treat them with respect, say thank you, apologise when it's your fault, pop by to say 'hi' when you visit the warehouse, give them the details they need. Try and treat them how you would want them to treat your customers.

eCommerce Business Structures – Key Challenges and Focuses

If you've followed the book *eCommerce MasterPlan: Your 3 Steps to Successful Online Selling* and identified your eCommerce business structure then here is where you should focus your delivery strategy effort on first:

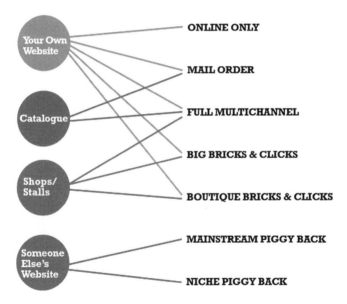

- Online Only, Mail Order, Boutique Bricks and Clicks:
  - You must find the right couriers.
  - And outsource your warehouse.
  - These are two of your most important relationships.

- Boutique Bricks and Clicks:
    - You must find the right couriers.
    - And make your parcels just as good as they are in-store.
- Big Bricks and Clicks, and Full Multichannel:
    - Leverage your store footprint for improved customer service.
    - Find the right couriers.
    - Maximise the potential of your parcel volume to get you good deals and services.
- PiggyBacking:
    - Keep an eye on what your competition are doing.
    - Consider Fulfilment by Amazon.
    - Test and tweak it.
    - Be careful what you put in the parcels – you don't want to fall foul of Amazon.

NOTES

What Next?

∙∙

If you've worked through the whole book you'll now know what your delivery strategy needs to be, so it's time to start implementing that. Start with Part 1 in order to increase your orders, then move on to Part 2, and finally make sure you've optimised your whole business with the tips in Part 3.

WORKBOOK
Don't forget to register at **eCommerceMasterPlan.com/Free** for your workbooks and other support materials.

Getting your delivery strategy right is going to really improve your business, but it doesn't mean you can put your feet up and stop learning (sorry!) – eCommerce and online marketing are still evolving so:

● Always keep optimising your business – identify the bit that is working the least well and improve it.
● Keep learning – watch out for new opportunities, new ideas and test them to see if they work for your business.

I am committed to keeping **eCommerceMasterPlan.com** up to date with the information the eCommerce business owner or marketer needs to know. It is simple, sensible advice. Visit today, subscribe to our emails and follow us on social media.

Then take a look at our other books available as ebooks and paperbacks.

Praise for eCommerce MasterPlan Books, Systems and Training

· ·

'With a knack for explaining complex business strategies and techniques in a straightforward, engaging manner, here's someone that any e-Commerce marketer, strategist or entrepreneur should be listening to.'

Power Retail Magazine

'I find Chloë's books and advice invaluable.'

Jim McDowell, Marketing Director, Sarah Raven

'Your book has saved my sanity and potential business – thank you from the bottom of my heart. I am currently working through the workbooks and am most appreciative of your way of getting to the essence of stuff, helping us to ask the right questions and enabling us as the managers of this process, not the technicians, to know what our strategy should be, what to manage, where the risks are and how to communicate and evaluate the technicians and suppliers.'

Izolde Bensch, eCommerce business owner, Australia

'Exactly what I needed – an easy roadmap to get me something I can visualise and achieve!'

Chantal Wellavize, eCommerce business owner UK, Equichoice

eCommerce MasterPlan 1.8: Your 3 Steps to Successful Online Selling

Buy now on Amazon:

http://ow.ly/zAhMT

eCommerce Marketing: How to Drive Traffic that Buys to Your Website

Buy now on Amazon:

http://ow.ly/zAigP

Find Out More About Chloë Thomas and eCommerce MasterPlan

. . . .

Just visit the website:

eCommerceMasterPlan.com

Take a look and connect on social media:

Pinterest:
www.pinterest.com/ChloeThomasECMP/

LinkedIn:
uk.linkedin.com/in/chloethomasecommerce/

Twitter:
twitter.com/Chloe_eCmp

Google+
plus.google.com/u/0/b/104640974802068228078/+Ecommercemas
terplan/posts

Facebook:
www.facebook.com/ecommercemasterplan

Or contact us an old-fashioned way:

e: Chloe@eCommerceMasterPlan.com
t: +44 (0) 1872 888 737
p: PO Box 740
Truro
TR1 9HE

We look forward to hearing from you!